PARASAUROLOPHUS

by
Mike Clark

PHOTO CREDITS

Abbreviations: l-left, r-right, b-bottom, t-top, c-center, m-middle.
Front Cover – Catmando. 2-3 background – Aqnus Febriyant. 2–3 front – Warpaint.
4-5 background – goory. 4 front – Catmando. 5 front – Warpaint. 6-7 – iurii.
8-9 background – kaesunza. 8l – MarcelClemens. 8r – guysal. 9 - Lisa Andres/
wikipedia. 11 front – Ralf Juergen Kraft. 11 back – Catmando. 12-13
background – ZoranKrstic. 12-13 front – Andreas Meyer. 14-15 – Catmando.
15 – D. Gordon E. Robertson. 16-17 – i am way. 16 – Catmando. 17 – topimages.
18-19l – Warpaint. 18-19m – Herschel Hoffmeyer. 18-19r - Warpaint. 20-21l – Ralf
Juergen Kraft. 20-21r – Luis Molinero. 24 – Catmando. All photos courtesy of
Shutterstock unless specified.

Published in 2018 by
KidHaven Publishing, an Imprint of Greenhaven Publishing, LLC
353 3rd Avenue
Suite 255
New York, NY 10010

Designer: Matt Rumbelow
Editor: Charlie Ogden

Cataloging-in-Publication Data

Names: Clark, Mike.
Title: Parasaurolophus / Mike Clark.
Description: New York : KidHaven Publishing, 2018. | Series: All about dinosaurs | Includes index.
Identifiers: ISBN 9781534523548 (pbk.) | 9781534523524 (library bound) | ISBN 9781534524668
(6 pack) | ISBN 9781534523531 (ebook)
Subjects: LCSH: Parasaurolophus–Juvenile literature. | Dinosaurs–Juvenile literature.
Classification: LCC QE862.O65 C53 2018 | DDC 567.914–dc23

Printed in the United States of America

CPSIA compliance information: Batch #CW18KL: For further information contact Greenhaven Publishing LLC, New York, New York at 1-844-317-7404.

Please visit our website, www.greenhavenpublishing.com. For a free color catalog of all our
high-quality books, call toll free 1-844-317-7404 or fax 1-844-317-7405.

CONTENTS

Words that appear like this can be found in the glossary on page 23.

WHAT WERE DINOSAURS?

Dinosaurs were reptiles that lived on Earth for more than 160 million years before they became extinct.

There were many different types of dinosaurs. They lived both on land and in water.

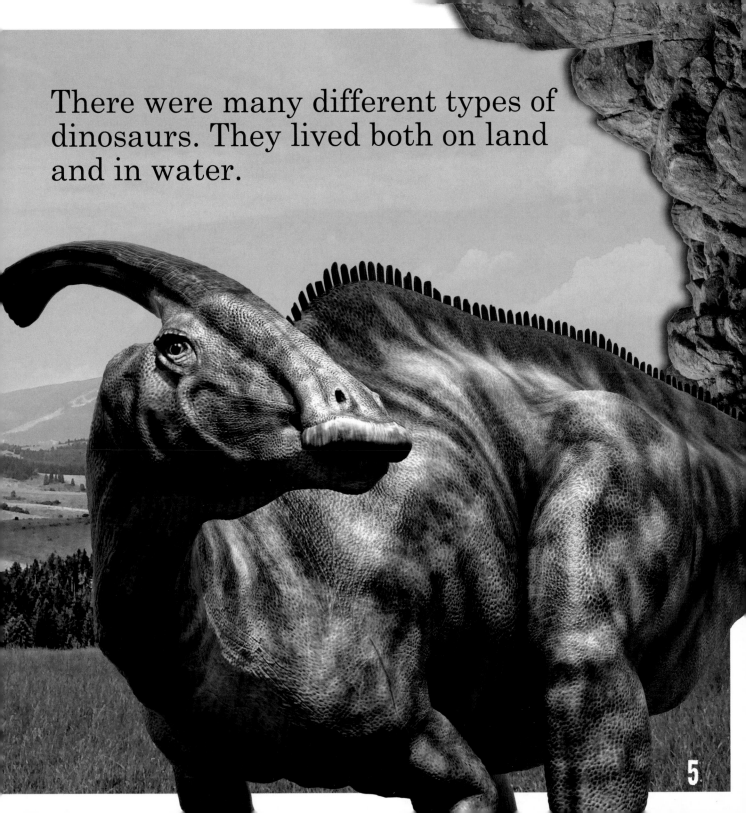

WHEN WERE DINOSAURS ALIVE?

Dinosaurs first roamed the earth around 230 million years ago during a period of time called the **Mesozoic** Era. The last dinosaurs went extinct around 65 million years ago.

Millions of years ago, all the land on Earth was together in one piece. However, during the time of the dinosaurs, it slowly broke up into the different **continents** that we know today.

WHEN ALL THE LAND ON EARTH WAS TOGETHER IN ONE PIECE, IT WAS CALLED PANGEA.

PANGEA

HOW DO WE KNOW...?

We know so much about dinosaurs thanks to scientists, called paleontologists, who study them. They dig up fossils of dinosaurs to find out more about them.

EGG

FOSSIL

Scientists put together the bones they find to try to make full dinosaur skeletons. From these skeletons, scientists can often find out the size of a dinosaur. We can also find out information about what it ate from its fossilized food and waste.

PARASAUROLOPHUS SKELETON

SCIENTISTS HAVE EVEN FOUND FOSSILIZED EGGS AND FOOTPRINTS BELONGING TO DINOSAURS.

PARASAUROLOPHUS

Parasaurolophus had one of the strangest skulls of any dinosaur. It had a large, horn-shaped bone sticking out of the back of its head. This is called a crest.

NAME	Parasaurolophus (par-uh-saw-ROL-uh-fuhs)
LENGTH	30 to 36 feet (9 to 11 m)
HEIGHT	11.4 feet (3.5 m)
WEIGHT	2.7 tons (2.5 mt)
FOOD	HERBIVORE
WHEN IT LIVED	65 to 76 million years ago
HOW IT MOVED	walked on both two and four legs at different times

Parasaurolophus lived more than 65 million years ago. It lived during the same time as *Albertosaurus*, which would have tried to eat *Parasaurolophus*.

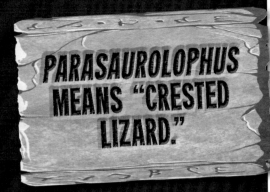

PARASAUROLOPHUS MEANS "CRESTED LIZARD."

ALBERTOSAURUS

CREST

WHAT DID PARASAUROLOPHUS LOOK LIKE?

Parasaurolophus had a thick tail that it used for balance. It sometimes stood on two legs to fight off **predators**, such as *Albertosaurus*.

12

Parasaurolophus also had a large crest on the back of its head. Paleontologists believe the crest might have helped the dinosaur to keep cool in hot weather.

WHERE DID PARASAUROLOPHUS LIVE?

Parasaurolophus fossils have been found in the United States and Canada. Paleontologists believe that these places were warm swamps during the time *Parasaurolophus* lived.

Canada

United States

Some paleontologists believe that Parasaurolophus lived in **herds**. Some paleontologists also think that groups of these dinosaurs moved huge distances during the year in order to stay in warm weather. This is known as migrating.

PARASAUROLOPHUS
SKULL

WHAT DID PARASAUROLOPHUS EAT?

Parasaurolophus was a herbivore, meaning that it only ate plants. It probably would have looked for food in swamps.

Parasaurolophus had large, flat teeth. It would have used these teeth to grind grass and leaves.

TEETH USED FOR EATING PLANTS

DID *PARASAUROLOPHUS* HAVE THE STRANGEST SKULL?

Parasaurolophus had a strange skull. However, it was not the only dinosaur with a strangely shaped head.

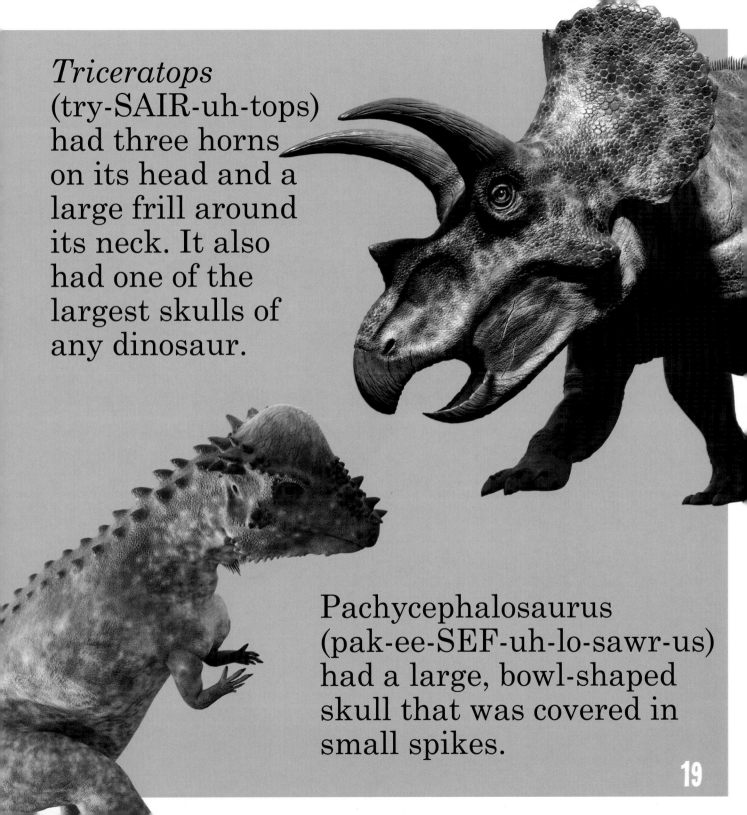

Triceratops (try-SAIR-uh-tops) had three horns on its head and a large frill around its neck. It also had one of the largest skulls of any dinosaur.

Pachycephalosaurus (pak-ee-SEF-uh-lo-sawr-us) had a large, bowl-shaped skull that was covered in small spikes.

A CLOSER LOOK AT PARASAUROLOPHUS

LARGE CREST

FLAT, GRINDING TEETH

6-FOOT (1.8 M) SKULL

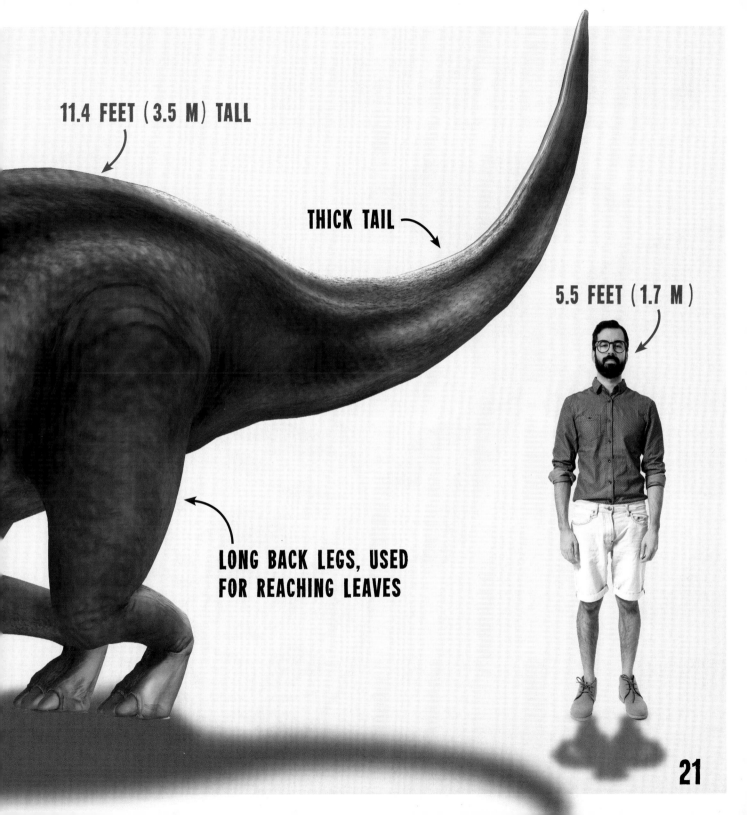

11.4 FEET (3.5 M) TALL

THICK TAIL

5.5 FEET (1.7 M)

LONG BACK LEGS, USED
FOR REACHING LEAVES

FIND ITS TWIN

GLOSSARY

continent   one of the seven great masses of land on Earth

extinct   no longer alive

fossil   the remains of old plants and animals that lived a long time ago

herbivore   an animal that only eats plants

herd   a large group of animals that live together

Mesozoic   a period of time when dinosaurs lived from 252.2 million years ago to 66 million years ago

predator   an animal that hunts other animals for food

reptile   a cold-blooded animal with scales

swamp   an area flooded with a shallow layer of water

INDEX